MW00625496

What Foster Parents Need to Know

Keeping a Journal, Handling Allegations,
Adoption Subsidies, and More

Revised Fifth Edition
Formerly *A Daily Journal for Foster Parents*

Created by Adoption in Child Time.

James A. Kenny, PhD, Editor

Copyright © 2015 Adoption in Child Time, Inc.
Published by the Brigittine Press.
All rights reserved.
ISBN: 978-0-9761564-5-1

TABLE OF CONTENTS

1
HOW TO KEEP A JOURNAL
Peter A. Kenny, Attorney

The strongest material you can have in advocating for your foster child is a well-documented daily journal. Keeping a daily journal assists you when reporting to the Child Welfare Department or advocating for your foster child at case conferences and at court hearings. When opinions are divided, your journal provides you with reasons and documentation for your views.

You can keep your journal on the Internet in a designated site or folder, in a simple inexpensive notebook, or even on scraps of paper to be typed into your Internet site or entered into your child's notebook later when it is more convenient. Be sure to write the date and the child's name at the start of each entry. This can be important should a dispute arise at a later time. It is best to keep a separate site or notebook for each child.

Judges can only make decisions about a child's case plan based on the information presented in court. The information, as presented by the Child Welfare Department or the birth parents, is often incomplete, biased, or just plain wrong. Your foster child depends on you as the most informed person in the courtroom to give the judge accurate information about his or her needs. Your journal can provide critical written evidence which can correct misinformation and bolster your position for what is in the child's best interests. Federal law states you have the right to present both written and oral evidence to the court. To help you get started, this article will include examples of journal entries.

Example: Joey, Jan. 16, 20___.
Joey's mother complained to the caseworker that we are
not giving him his meds. I explained to the caseworker that
the doctor changed Joey's meds at the last visit and we are
following the new schedule.

Include everything in your journal, the more information the better. You never know what problems may develop. Here are some situations where a daily journal is extremely helpful:

1. You may need to defend yourself against a false allegation of abuse or neglect.
2. You may feel that a proposed visitation with a particular person would be harmful to the child.
3. You may be pursuing an adoption which one or both birth parents are contesting.
4. You want to prepare a Life Book recording all that you know about your foster child's past and present.

Write on a regular basis, daily or at least every few days. Set a regular time to write and stick to it. If you decide to write "when you get around to it," the days will fly by and nothing will be recorded. Be sure to write when your foster child has had some special event in his or her life.

Example: Joey, Feb 13, 20___.
Joey's school held a presentation for parents today.
Joey read part of a paragraph. He spoke up well and did
an excellent job. I got a picture of him during the
performance.

Do not use your journal to attack the birth parents, the Child Welfare Department or any other interested parties. Instead pretend you are a camera, and record what happened each day. Did the child cry, laugh, get angry, act out, appear sad?

Example: Joey, Feb. 15, 20___.
Joey and William got into a fight after dinner tonight.

My husband Bob bundled Joey and himself up and took him out for a walk. I got William working on his homework. After half an hour both boys had calmed down and by bedtime they were able to sleep.

Describe any actions of the child which influence your judgment: failing to eat; unexplained sickness or vomiting; fighting with another child in the household; destructive behavior of any kind.

Example: Joey, Feb 25, 20___.
Last night Joey had a nightmare. He started to cry and holler around midnight. I went to him and he started to sob and cling to me. I held him until he calmed down. Then we went to the kitchen and I gave him a glass of milk. He drank it and said he was ready to go back to bed.

Example: Joey, Mar 1, 20___.
William complained that he had five dollars on the night stand by his bed and it disappeared. I found five dollars under a book on Joey's desk this afternoon when I was cleaning. I told both boys that I could not prove exactly what happened, but that I would check both rooms regularly and that I would not respect their privacy until this matter settled down. I don't know whether this problem is solved. I'll stay alert and keep working on it.

Describe the good things as well: school successes, kindnesses, good interactions with peers. Remember....facts, not feelings.

Example: Joey, Mar 4, 20___.
Tonight after dinner the kids decided to play UNO. Joey joined in and seemed to enjoy it. He didn't win, but that didn't upset him as it has after previous games.

Start today to keep a journal. Your foster child needs your input.

2
QUARTERLY SUMMARY OUTLINE
(for case conferences and court hearings)

Summarize your journal entries every three months in writing to inform the judge at a court review hearing, to update your caseworker, or simply to organize your own thinking about your foster child. The documented written word usually carries more weight than oral testimony alone.

NAME OF CHILD _____

DATE _____

GENERAL: Tell what has gone well with your foster child. Tell any problems that need to be addressed.

SCHOOL: Record your foster child's grades and behavior.

MEDICAL: Note any illnesses, injuries, or medical problems. Give dates of doctor visits.

DENTAL AND EYE CARE: List any visits to the dentist or optometrist and write of results.

COUNSELING: List visits to the therapist and tell of your foster child's progress.

FOSTER HOME: Tell how your foster child has adjusted and gotten along in your home.

SOCIAL SKILLS: Tell how your foster child has gotten along with others his/her age.

SPECIAL INTERESTS: Note any activities or hobbies that your foster child enjoys.

VISITATION: List visits with the birth family and tell how they have gone.

CASEWORKER: Describe your relationship with the Division of Family and Children.
What issues would you like to discuss at the next case conference?

ANYTHING ELSE that you believe is important.

SIGNATURE OF FOSTER PARENT _____

3
WHY AND HOW TO PREPARE A LIFE BOOK
Tom and Jean Gaunt (Biological, adoptive, and foster parents)

Life Books create connections. Connections with our past are what give us our identity, stability, wholeness, a sense of permanence. Connections allow us to enter new relationships as a complete person, without feeling so lost and adrift, without feeling empty.

Connections are relationships, memories, feelings, places, and things that make up the fabric of belonging to and being a part of a family or a group. Connections are essential to us because they help define who we are and help provide the foundation for our wellbeing.

When a disconnection happens it can impact who we are and how we feel about ourselves. When several disconnections occur, they often have severe adverse effects on our self-esteem and wellbeing. Think of it this way...

As adults we are connected in many ways. We usually have a job, may go to church, attend various organizations, be a family member, enjoy personal possessions, own property, maintain a home, and have friends and neighbors. Okay, now think about being awakened from your sleep in the middle of the night by strangers and being taken away from everything that is important to you. Everything that is important to you is a connection. How would you feel — scared, resentful, distrustful, lost, or angry? ...and maybe you'd become depressed or develop anxiety?

Now think about a child that is removed from his or her home, abruptly leaving behind relationships, familiar places, and personal possessions – clothes, toys, special items, grandma and grandpa, brothers and sisters, friends, playmates, school, teachers, church, and on and on...

And then... the child moves from foster home to foster home, and maybe back home or on to an adoptive home. Each move creates even more disconnections.

Disconnection happens. It's a fact of life. No one enjoys having to remove a child from his or her home. Foster and adoptive parents can play an important role in helping to maintain, reconnect, or create new connections for their foster or adoptive child. A Life Book is one important way of maintaining and reconnecting with old relationships and of creating new ones.

If your foster child is returning to the birth home, you want to maintain and honor as many home connections as you are allowed. Simple connections that make a difference for children are continuing their religious tradition, maintaining the parent's preference for their child's hair style, and including the child's favorite types of food at dinner. In this case, the Life Book would be a collection of pictures, impressions, and feelings collected during the period they were placed in your home.

If you are adopting a foster child or are the foster parent of a child that is being adopted, Life Books help prepare the foster child for adoption. Help your child collect pictures, record memories, and write down his or her feelings. This allows the connection process to begin. The child's past will always be a part of who they are and the Life Book provides an appropriate way to help frame their past in context with their new family.

Use a standard binder with a clear pocket cover. Let your foster/adoptive child design the insert for the front cover. You should also include envelopes in the back of the binder for your child to collect keepsakes. This provides an opportunity for your child to claim ownership of their Life Book. Work with your child and be creative!

(You can download this outline from the following URL: www.adoptioninchildtime.org/abdownloads)

Chapter One: Who Me?
    a) Baby pictures
    b) Important information like a copy of the birth certificate, birth information (hospital, date of birth, weight, length), social security number, etc.
    c) Questions to be answered. What is my favorite food? What do I want to be when I grow up? What makes me happy? What makes me angry?

Chapter Two: My Birth Family
    a) Include as many pictures as possible of birth relatives such as mom and dad, grandparents, aunts and uncles, siblings, and others. If no pictures are available, then provide space for your child to draw pictures of their family.
    b) Make a family tree.
    c) Take a trip and take pictures with your child of their birth homes, schools, play areas and fun spots.
    d) Ask them to write down feelings about their birth family. What was your favorite family holiday? What do you miss about your birth home? What would you say to your birth parents?
    e) This chapter could include a letter to their birth parents saying good bye.

Chapter Three: My Schools
    a) A place for each school grade picture
    b) A listing of schools attended
    c) Pictures of teachers or class pictures
    d) An art picture for each grade
    e) Report cards

Chapter Four: What Makes Me Tick?
    a) Shot records
    b) Medical history
    c) List of doctors and professional service providers
    d) Family medical history
    e) Special needs

Chapter Five: Getting Adopted!?!?
a) Listing and pictures of previous foster parents
b) Questions to answer before meeting adoptive parents. Where would I like to live? What do I think my adoptive parents will be like? What would I like my bedroom to be like?
c) Questions to answer after moving in. Date when I met my new adoptive parents? Date when I moved in? Date my adoption was finalized?
d) Pictures of my new family and me!

Memories provide us with a base. We need a base from which to grow. That is what a Life Book does: It provides the displaced child with the story of his or her journey. Where he can go depends on where he's been. Give your child the gift of his or her past.

4

THERE'S NO PLACE LIKE A PERMANENT HOME

James A. Kenny, PhD

Imagine yourself on a trip. You have just learned that your house with everything in it has burned to the ground. Where will you go? What shall you do? Imagine yourself homeless in a big city. You live in a cardboard box. If it gets too cold, you must try to find food and a shelter. The shelters are full and you move from one to the next. Imagine yourself a refugee. A hurricane has flooded and destroyed your home. You are on a bus headed somewhere, you don't know where. Or you are in a war zone. Your home has been destroyed. Your family is missing, perhaps dead. You are wandering around, don't know where you are supposed to go. Nobody wants you.

Foster parents in training are sometimes asked to write down the ten people or things they value most on separate slips of paper. Then they are asked to give up one, throw it in the trash basket, and discuss their loss. One by one, they are asked to get rid of what they value, till finally they arrive at the last treasure. Give that up too. And that is how a foster child feels when he first comes to your house.

Take that situation one step further. Time drags on in the new home but nothing happens. The child becomes attached and so does the foster parent. But still nothing happens to suggest permanence. The child wonders if anyone really cares enough to make a family commitment.

The foster parent may want the child to stay, but bureaucracy and unending fruitless reunifications continue. The child is removed, shuffled around, loses people he or she had come to trust, reaches out to people that disappear. No matter how cogent and rational the explanations, the child knows better. He fantasizes: "If you really loved me, you would keep me. No one loves me. I am not worth much. I can't trust anyone. I will never have a place called home."

Delay is child abuse. We know the consequences of delay, both from psychological research and from the law. We know the harm that can result from drifting along in foster care. Yet too often the state moves from abuse by the birth parents to further abuse by the very systems that were designed to protect the child, the welfare departments and courts.

The research shows that bonding is likely after three months, probable after six, and almost certain after 12 months. Interrupted bonding takes a heavy physical and emotional toll. For these reasons, the law allows for a change in the permanency plan after six months, and requires that a termination of parental rights be filed after 12-15 months.

So why do we fail to show the urgency that the research and laws insist upon? No matter what the reason, time without a resolution sends a message to the child in care: "No one really wants you. You must not be a good person."

There are several reasons why children remain in limbo. Some delays are systemic. The caseworker is too busy to set up the case plan, visit the home, or prepare for a court hearing. The courts allow continuances because the parties have not been properly notified, a more compelling matter must be heard, or the attorneys have a scheduling conflict.

Other reasons are given. Blood is thicker than water. Every effort must be made to find a biological relative. This makes good sense at the start, when the child is removed from the parental home and first placed. As time passes, however, new relationships are fashioned. Bonding may take place.

Bonding outweighs kinship. Significant psychological connections are real and vital, and they are more important than mere blood relations. The marriage bond is not a blood relationship but it is an example of a significant attachment that supersedes biological relationships. When the child has bonded, with his or her long-time foster parent and they wish to adopt, this should take precedence over a heretofore unknown relative.

Another reason sometimes given by caseworkers and courts to delay is that getting it right takes time. "We must wait until we are sure we have it right." That is a mistake. No matter how "right" the final resolution may appear, a sure way to get things wrong is to wait. While the system waits, the child is growing and developing, both physically and psychologically. Waiting is destructive.

"Older children should be allowed to choose whether they want to be adopted." This is a tough one. The teen must have a voice. Yet we know that most 14-year-olds have a very naïve idea of how the world works, what it takes to survive as an adult. They may brashly want to be free of any parental controls. They may have a hope of being reunited to an idealized birth parent, having forgotten the neglect and abuse they earlier experienced. The birth home may remain the only "true" home they have known. Or they may be reacting with rejection to the fact that they have felt rejected.

A wise foster parent who is offering a forever home through adoption must be patient and not force the issue. Stress the value of a lifetime connection, a place to which one can always return. Every person has the right and need for a permanent home, even when, for the moment, they feel otherwise. Offer the chance for continuing contact with the birth parents though a cooperative adoption.

So what can be done to hasten the process without jeopardizing good sense? Knowing that waiting can be harmful, how can we avoid delay and still get it right? Here are four strong suggestions:

1. Follow the laws and policies. In practice, federal and state laws set a limit of one year in which to find the child a permanent home, either through reunification or adoption. Take that mandate seriously. A year is already a long time in the life of a child.

2. Begin at once. The caseworker should give the birth parents a reunification plan within 48 hours following the removal of the child. This is not hard. What is the plan? It is a direct response to the very reasons for removal. The plan can be revised as more information becomes available. A concerned birth parent would be happy to know how to get their child back and would start at once. An immediate case plan may include any or all of the following, with deadlines:

a. Health of Birth Parent. Medical evaluation and/or treatment; Mental health evaluation and/or treatment; Drug screening; AA attendance; etc.

b. Change of Residence. Move to acceptable housing; Separate from abusive person; etc.

c. Employment. Show number of jobs applied for; Obtain a job; Hold a job for ____ weeks; etc.

d. Parent Training. Classes; Observation time with foster parent; Volunteer time at daycare center, etc.

e. Visitation. When? Where? How often?

3. Follow up. The caseworkers should set deadlines for the completion of each task and check regularly. If the birth parents accomplish their tasks, that hastens reunification. If not, that may be evidence for termination. Delays may occur because the birth parents are unable or fail to accomplish the required tasks in a timely manner. Delays must not stem from the caseworker failing to give the birth parents an immediate reunification plan or from a failure to check if deadlines are met. Birth parents must know specifically what they need to do from the start, and then must be held accountable.

4. Zero tolerance for delays. The child's rights are paramount. Delays are a form of child abuse. Every effort must be made by the welfare system and the courts to avoid delays. Delays should not be granted for the mere convenience of the adults, but only for the most serious and unavoidable reasons.

Children in foster care are adrift without a firm base. Too often the attitude is that they are just children. They have a roof over their head. They are being fed. They are attending school. They are physically safe and secure. So what's the problem? Children need more than a warehouse. They need a permanent home within a reasonable time. They need to belong somewhere. We all do.

Children are our most valuable resource, our hope for the future. Foster children are our most vulnerable citizens. Concern for their well-being must have the highest priority. Delays in establishing permanence hurt the foster child. Every child has the right to a permanent home within a reasonable time.

5
LEGAL DEFINITIONS OF BONDING

Mark Bontrager, J.D. and James Kenny, PhD
(From "Fostering Families Today": May/June, 2004)

More and more, the courts are becoming aware of the critical importance of bonding. In the past, courts weighed biological connections heavily and may have allowed this factor to overshadow the bonding that takes place when people live together for an extended time and "act" as a family. The recognition of bonding and continuity of care as significant factors in contested adoptions should provide guidance for trial court judges.

For the court to decide that bonding is critical, it must first be able to recognize bonding when it occurs. Too often bonding has remained a fuzzy concept, a feel-good term to highlight the presence of mutual affection and positive regard. In fact, bonding can be defined in a factual and evidentiary way. The court needs to know when and how bonding occurs, and what happens when it is interrupted.

Definition

Bonding is a significant reciprocal attachment which both parties want and expect to continue, and which is interrupted or terminated at considerable peril to the parties involved. Human beings bond by sharing everyday vital life events in daily life, such as eating, sleeping, and playing together. Bonding takes time. Research shows that it is likely after three months, probable after six, and almost certain after 12 months. The earlier in life that the bonded relationship is interrupted, the more serious are the consequences.

What Happens When Bonded Relationships Are Interrupted?

Psychopathology, now or in later adult life, is a statistically significant possibility. A child who has been separated from someone he or she depends on and loves may be afraid to bond or love again. Even more serious, as adults he or she may be unable to feel compassion or to form and maintain personal relationships.

Interrupting bonded relationships takes a heavy toll on human health and well-being. Such a severance can rightly be labeled social surgery, akin to and as serious as brain surgery, divorce, or death. The younger the child and the deeper the bond, the more devastating can be the result.

Interrupted bonding has commonly been listed as a major or contributing cause to psychiatric disorders in children. These include Reactive Attachment Disorder, Attention Deficit Disorder (AD/HD), Oppositional Defiant Disorder (ODD), Adjustment Disorders, Learning Disorders, and Developmental Delay.

The research shows that interrupted bonding can also lead to later and more serious adult disorders. Over 50 percent of **homeless** adults were once shuffled around in foster care. The loss of bonded relationships has been shown to be a significant factor in **mental illness**, including most psychotic and neurotic disorders. Interrupted bonding has been significantly linked to adult **crime**. Multiply-placed and separated children are psychopaths in the making. Finally, children who are separated from the significant care persons often end up in **poverty**.

Bonding Is Primary

Bonding should take precedence over kinship. Bonding is kinship. Strong relationships and potential lifetime commitments are more valuable to the child than blood ties.

The marriage relationship is one example of the precedence of bonding over blood ties. If bonding is so important, why have the courts not always seen matters that way?

An obvious answer to this question is that bonding has rarely been defined in a specific evidentiary way that can be presented as fact rather than opinion. The Child Welfare Manual of the Indiana Division of Family and Children provided four excellent criteria, based on a considerable body of research, any one of which is sufficient to determine whether bonding has occurred. These criteria are the Length of Time, the Behavior of the Child, the Reciprocal Attachment, and Family identification.

Time in place is one factual way to measure bonding. In a parent-child setting, bonding is likely after three months, probable after six, and almost certain after one year. Research indicates that three months is the usual length of time that human beings take to adjust to any new or different situation. Normal children will attach well within six months. The federal Adoption and Safe Families Act (ASFA, 1997) reflects this research by setting one year as a deadline for filing termination of parental rights.

The **behavior of the child** is a second way to determine whether bonding has occurred. Bonded children seek to stay close to the parent. They turn to the parent when frightened or hurt. They may object when the parent leaves them. They copy the parent's mannerisms. They want the parent to watch and admire what they do. Bonding checklists can be used to measure these behaviors clinically.

Bonding is **reciprocal**. It works both ways. The strength of the parent's commitment can be determined. The bonded parent wants to be the forever parent. The bonded parent wants to raise the child, to be there through homework battles and broken hearts, through the first car and the first job, through the child's marriage, through job loss or divorce, through joy and heartbreak until death. Bonds are meant to be permanent.

Family identification is a fourth way to measure bonding. The evaluator should explore whether and in what way the child identifies himself as a member of the foster/adopt family. Check with the community, the school, friends, neighbors, and extended family members, to determine how and whether the child is perceived as a member of the foster/adopt family. Has the child developed self-reliance and a trust of the foster family?

Community consensus is akin to our jury system whereby the court trusts the collective wisdom about a critical matter. A good evaluator will explore and assess what those people think who know the child and his or her attachments best. What evidence can be offered to determine where this child truly belongs?

Pseudo -Bonding and Other Myths

While many people understand what is meant by bonding, the process has too often been misunderstood to the peril of the children and the families involved. The heretofore vague and "feel-good" definitions of bonding have given rise to several myths.

Some naïve persons believe that the child who has bonded well to one family is a "good bonder" and will do equally well if moved to another family. It may even happen that the child is pleasant and compliant and shows no overt signs of distress. This is rightly called pseudo-bonding and reflects the very opposite of bonding. The compliance is very often a superficial veneer, covering a lack of attachment, which may well show up in adult life as psychopathology.

Humans do not bond nor love generically. We bond to the specific person in this place. Suppose you have been happily married for two years when the kind and well-meaning person in charge of your life announces: "Tonight you will be going home to a different husband. He is a very nice man and lives in a very nice place." Crazy? No more so than telling a foster child that he will be happy moving to a new placement.

A second myth suggests that no harm is done when an infant or very young child is moved from home to home because they will not remember the experience later. Completely erroneous. The earlier a consequential event occurs in life, the more it determines future patterns of adjustment. Separation and loss are always consequential events. If separation and loss are hard for an adult, they are catastrophic for a small child.

Still another myth suggests that bonding is a skill. Parents and children can both learn how to be "good attachers." Of course people can learn to become socially skilled. Any good salesman has mastered the techniques of connecting in order to make a sale. This is not what is meant by bonding. In a related vein, foster parents are often counseled not to become too attached to the children in their care. Wrong again. Bonding is what happens to normal people of all ages when they share meals and bedtime stories, chores and recreation, videos and baseball games and TV cartoons. Bonding is part of the process of living.

ASFA, with its research-based deadlines for requiring permanent homes for children, has led the way. The courts at all levels are becoming open to the concept and importance of bonding. Caseworkers, CASAs, parents, foster parents, and attorneys now all bear the responsibility of seeing that bonding is presented to the court in a well-defined and thorough fashion.

Presenting Bonding to the Court

1. If you are a foster parent who has had a child with you for one year or more and you wish to adopt, hire an attorney. Not just any attorney but one who is experienced and knowledgeable about the complicated process of foster care adoptions.

2. The attorney can help you through the prerequisite termination of parental rights (TPR.) If the adoption is to be disputed, you may want to file for adoption even before the TPR to insure that you will be a legal party and have an equal voice in court.

3. Hire a psychologist who is knowledgeable about bonding and experienced with court testimony. You need an expert witness to convince the court of the presence of bonding and the perils of ignoring it. Your expert should be

familiar with the bonding research. .

4. Here are some other rather obvious but important points that should be presented to the court:

(1) One year is a long time in the life of a child. ASFA's guidelines are important and should be followed.

(2) Foster care is (or should be) temporary. Foster care must not become a way of life.

(3) Reunification and adoption are the only two truly permanent solutions. While ASFA allows for kin care and "permanent" legal guardianship as alternate permanency plans, neither are a permanent solution.

(4) All children have the right to a permanent home. The primary consideration should not be the rights of the adult but the best interest and rights of the child. As ASFA makes explicit, the rights of the child are paramount.

The courts at all levels have begun to recognize the importance of bonding as it relates to kinship. To make their case, foster parents who wish to adopt must engage an attorney who is knowledgeable and experienced in adoptions from foster care and an expert witness who can evaluate and define bonding in a way that will be convincing.

6

A VOICE FOR FOSTER PARENTS

James A. Kenny, PhD

ACT (www.adoptioninchildtime.org) believes that every child has the right to a permanent home. Reunification and adoption are the only two true permanent resolutions.

Foster parenting involves more than providing food and shelter for a child in wardship. Advocating for the foster child is one of the rights and duties of a foster parent. The foster parent is responsible for the child 24/7, and in that circumstance, often knows the child's current situation better than anyone else.

Suppose, for example, you object to certain portions of the case plan. You believe that what has been proposed is not in the child's best interests. You may disagree with the visitation agreement or with requirements for counseling or for placement in special education classes. You may disagree with the decision to remove the child from your home for reasons other than substantiated abuse. As a team member, a professional and trained parent and an advocate for the child in your care, you have the duty to make your voice heard. The following rights should assist you in fulfilling that duty.

The right to call a case conference

Foster parents are to be involved in decisions about placement of their foster children and about developing or changing the case plan. Should a caseworker plan to remove a child from the foster home for reasons other than substantiated abuse, and the foster parent disagrees, the foster parent should be able to call for a case conference to include the caseworker, the foster parents, the birth parents, the CASA, and the child if appropriate. Additional persons of import such as teachers and counselors may also be invited. Every effort should be made to achieve agreement.

The right to hire an attorney

Foster parents may seek the services of an attorney to represent their position at case conferences, appeals hearings, and in court.

The right to notification of all periodic case reviews

Ten days before the periodic case review, including a case review that is a permanency hearing, the state should provide notice of the hearing to the child's foster parent.

The right to submit a written statement directly to the court

The foster parent should be able to submit his or her daily journal about the child's progress, or any other documentation or statement directly to the judge. This might include the identification of persons, such as relatives, teachers, therapists, and others who know the child and whom the court might wish to hear before making a life-shaping decision. Such written material can be made a part of the court record, provided that a copy has been given to the other parties in the proceeding.

The right to present oral testimony in court

In addition to presenting a written statement, the foster parent(s) should also have the opportunity to address the court as a witness to testify about the child's well-being and what the foster parent perceives to be in the child's best interests.

The right to cross-examine all witnesses at the hearing

The foster parents should have the right to cross-examine any witnesses at the court review or permanency hearings. This would include the caseworker, therapist, teachers, anyone who gives testimony. Probably, the foster parents would wish to be represented by an attorney who would perform the cross-examinations.

The right to request intervention as a legal party

In addition to the above rights, legal party status would give foster parents the right to file motions. Foster parents have always had the right to request party status. The judge may grant such standing if he or she deems it to be in the child's best interests.

Conclusions

To promote permanence and other vital child-rearing outcomes, foster parents need guaranteed rights of access to the child welfare agencies and the courts, those parties who make the important decisions. These rights are not about new privileges for foster parents. Rather, they represent the opportunity for foster parents to fulfill one of their important duties: to act as advocate for the children in their care. The best interests of the child require that foster parents have the opportunity to tell the court fully what they know and what they are willing to provide, before the court decides the child's entire future.

7

MAKING YOUR VOICE COUNT
James A. Kenny, PhD

"I don't think that the family therapy is helping," said one foster parent. "We all have to go three times a week. We'd do better if it were changed or stopped. But I'm afraid to bring it up or argue for fear we'll have our foster children removed – or be blackballed from any more placements."

In addition to counseling, foster parents often have something to say about medical care, school issues, visitation with the birth parents, and whether and when to change the permanency plan to adoption. Their knowledge and opinions need to be heard. But unfortunately, they are too often afraid to speak out.

Foster children would benefit from an honest discussion of alternatives. Yet, the foster parents may feel they are "just foster parents," or that they are not important decision-makers. Although the 1997 federal Adoption and Safe Families Act (ASFA) said foster parents should be heard in court, too often they are afraid to speak their minds for fear of retaliation.

Four players usually manage the decision-making process. Three of the players, the caseworker, court-appointed special advocate (CASA), and the judge, have real power. The fourth player, the birth parents, can guarantee the return of their child by complying with the guidelines set forth by the welfare department and the court. Foster parents, the fifth players, have no formal power.

Yet foster parents are the only players who have 24/7 day-after-day knowledge of the children in their home. They know and they care and they must have input. However, because of their lack of formal power, they must use other strategies to make their recommendations known and to influence the decisions that shape a child's entire future.

Getting along is a good strategy for being heard and getting one's way. Since foster parents cannot mandate decisions, and are not likely to win any heads-on confrontation, they need to find a way to work together with the caseworker and CASA.

Caving in meekly to what the others recommend or being silent in fear of retaliation should not be an option. Rather, foster parents must learn how to present their knowledge and opinions without threatening the other players. One does not have to be confrontational to be effective.

Knowledge is power, and therein lies the foster parents' elemental strength. They must find productive ways to present this everyday knowledge about the child to those who make the critical decisions. Foster parents cannot mandate or order their information to be implemented. Rather, they must act as salesmen in presenting what they know and believe.

Here are nine rules that will help foster parents advocate more effectively for the youngsters under their care.

1. Communicate with your caseworker on a regular, even weekly, basis. Don't wait for a crisis. Stay in touch. A phone call, a mailed journal update, or an email may be sufficient. Build a normal and steady routine of contact.

2. Keep a daily journal. Record school successes and failures, medical concerns and doctor appointments, and positive and negative behavior. Note how visitation with the birth parents went. You may add your own opinions and judgments, but keep these separate from the factual information.

3. Begin all communications on a positive note. Learn to begin with at least two positive remarks. Every face-to-face contact with the other players should start with two uncritical comments or compliments. This tried-and-true strategy is used in mediation, labor-management negotiations, and in sales. Praise their office décor or what they are wearing. Offer a smile. Ask a question about something of theirs that you notice, perhaps a family picture or a sports trophy. Thank them for inviting you.

4. Use "I" messages. All good communication must be informative. You are an expert on what you think and feel, not what you suspect the other person thinks. Practice using "I" instead of "you" in your discussions. The "I" message avoids criticism and judgments about positions other than your own. People are more apt to hear what you have to say if you don't spend your time criticizing their contributions.

5. Listen. Keep your mind open. Consider what others have to offer. Respect their thinking. People are more likely to listen to you if you listen to them.

6. Work regularly with the CASA. Keep them informed of the everyday progress and setbacks along with the caseworker. Use the same communication techniques.

7. Work with the birth parents. Remember, reunification must be the initial goal. Treat them with courtesy, cooperate with visitation, and help them learn how to parent when possible. They can make good allies if later you wish to adopt the child.

8. Stand up for your child. State what you think is best and why. Don't blame or impugn the motives of others. Find a way to get your information to the caseworker and, if necessary, into court before the judge. Don't be hesitant for fear of being blackballed. Remember, the best decisions can only be made if all sides and opinions are adequately presented.

9. Regard court as a last resort. The courtroom is an adversarial setting. Arguing in court may sometimes be necessary, but it is far better to have matters resolved beforehand. If you feel you will have problems presenting important information in court, hire an attorney who is familiar with foster care policies and laws.

In Summary

If foster parents wish to make a difference, then the key is getting along. Use your communication skills to be sure that the information necessary to make informed decisions affecting the child's entire life and future is available to the welfare department and in court.

Then, if you still feel strongly that the child's best interests are being ignored, follow through with your role as advocate. Hire an attorney to be sure your information and recommendations are fully presented before the judge.

The child in your care needs your knowledge and love. He needs you to stand up for him. Do your very best to get along with those in power. But if you cannot, then stay the course to be fully heard. The child is the most important party to all these efforts, and the child's best interests are paramount.

8
ADOPTION SUBSIDIES
James A. Kenny, PhD

Many different subsidies are available for foster parents who wish to adopt. These subsidies offer an incentive to provide permanence. Continuing financial assistance is possible in five different packages. They include continuing the monthly payments of per diem, health insurance through Medicaid, reimbursement for expenses incurred by the adoption, a federal income tax credit, and college tuition. Your new child is entitled to all the financial support that is offered.

The North American Council on Adoptable Children (NACAC) is the best source for accurate information on the many and differing subsidies available in each of the 50 states. NACAC believes that adoption assistance is vital for families raising children with serious behavioral, emotional, or physical disabilities. Because of their commitment, they welcome individual and personal questions about adoption assistance.

Since 1994, NACAC has operated the Adoption Subsidy Resource Center to educate parents and professionals about the benefits available to children and youth adopted from foster care. Profiles on each of the state subsidy programs are provided. In addition, NACAC offers definitions of special needs, and fact sheets on various aspects relating to post-adoption support programs.

Contact NACAC's Adoption Subsidy Resource Center at 800-470-6665. E-mail to adoption.assistance@nacac.org. Website: www.nacac.org.

1. Continuing the Monthly Payments of Per Diem

Under the Title IV-E Adoption Assistance program (Title IV AA), the federal and state governments work together in an effort to continue and try to match the monthly reimbursement the foster child received prior to adoption. The purpose is to assure that a family with their newly adopted child does not suffer financially because of their willingness to provide a permanent home. Unfortunately, some states will try not to match the rate and offer as little as possible. In this case, negotiating is critical. Post-adoption per diem can continue until age 18, and in some special cases, be extended till age 21.The IRS does not count this Adoption Subsidy as income.

To be eligible for most subsidies, the child must qualify as having special needs. While the states define special needs in various and confusing ways, the overall meaning is relatively clear. A child with special needs is one who is "hard to place." The qualifying definition may be thought of as simple as 1-2-3.

One, the rights of the birth parents must have been terminated. Two, the child must be more difficult to adopt because of age, belonging to a sibling group, or having a diagnosed medical or psychological problem. Three, the state must have made a "reasonable effort" to find a family willing to adopt the child without any subsidy. An exception is made to this third condition, however, if moving to another family is not in the child's best interests. This condition may arise if the child has a significant emotional bond with foster parents who want to adopt or a relative is willing to adopt.

While still considered to have special needs, some children may not have been eligible for federal monies. In these cases, State Non-Title IV-E funds may fill in the gap. Every state seems to have a different definition or approach to adoption assistance. NACAC provides state profiles and will respond to individual questions about local eligibility for subsidies. (www.nacac.org/adoptionsubsidy/stateprofiles.html)

2. Medicaid

Children who have a federally funded AA subsidy are automatically eligible for Medicaid benefits. For foster/adopted children who are not eligible for IV-E AA, an agreement may include Medicaid, depending on the rules of the state that enters into the agreement. Interstate adoptions can become very complicated and may require the assistance of NACAC and a knowledgeable attorney.

Continuing Medicaid coverage is critical for most children who are adopted from foster care. You also need to make certain ahead of time that your child will continue to be covered by Medicaid. Even after approval, however, coverage can continue to be a problem. It may be difficult to find out which health care providers accept your type of Medicaid. Coverage may cease when the State switches you from one private contracted provider to another that does not pay for your type of Medicaid. In addition to NACAC, a good source of local information about how to handle these problems will be your fellow foster/adoptive parents.

3. Adoption Expenses (NRAE)

Federal monies are available for reimbursement of non-recurring adoption expenses up to $2000. These are one-time expenses directly related to the adoption of a child with special needs. They may include attorney fees, home study fees, replacement of the birth certificate, and travel to and from the child, including mileage, lodging and meals. In many states, the prospective adoptive parents are required to hire their own attorney, and frequently those attorneys charge what is allowed by NRAE. Some states may pay the attorney directly so that the family does not have to pay out of pocket and be reimbursed later.

4. Federal Income Tax Credit

Since 2003, families who adopted a child with special needs from foster care could claim a federal adoption tax credit even if they had no adoption expenses. Children who receive adoption assistance/subsidy benefits are considered children with special needs. Other adoptive families are also eligible for the credit, but must have (and be able to document, if requested by the IRS) qualified adoption expenses. The tax credit was refundable for 2010 and 2011, but not for 2012 or future years. A refundable tax credit is one you get back regardless of what you owe or paid in taxes for the year. When the credit is not refundable, you can only use up to what you have in federal income tax liability. Any unmet amount of the credit can be carried forward to the next tax year for up to six years. After that, the tax credit will disappear. In recent years (2011 to 2014) tax credits of up to $13,000 have been allowed. This is a one-time credit for adoption. (www.nacac.org/taxcredit/taxcredit.html)

5. College Assistance

Children adopted from foster care at age 13 or older can apply as an independent student for FAFSA (Free Application for Federal Student Aid). Children adopted from foster care after their 16th birthday can be eligible for Education and Training vouchers. Some states have tuition-waiver programs for children adopted from foster care. The amount of tuition waived is typically the in-state amount for state colleges and universities in the state where the child was adopted. NACAC has a fact sheet on the different state college tuition programs. (www.nacac.org/adoptionsubsidy/factsheets/tuition.html)

Negotiating Subsidy Rates and Other Entitlements

Federal Law states: "The amount of the payments to be made in any case....shall be determined through agreement between the adoptive parents and the state or local agency administering the program....which shall take into consideration the circumstances of the adopting parents and the needs of the child being adopted, and may be adjusted periodically, with the concurrence of the adopting parents....depending upon changes in such circumstances."

Some states offer the maximum which is the appropriate

foster care rate for the child's current needs. Other states begin the negotiations by offering zero. This may be understandable as they believe they are saving the state money. However, you need to know the maximum to which your child may be entitled. In most states, once you have the adoption subsidy, the amount can be renegotiated later if there is a new diagnosis or a change in family circumstances. A few states will not allow a family to renegotiate to a new maximum even if the child's needs have greatly increased.

It is in your child's best interest to ask for the maximum rate. The state may argue that if you really loved this child, you wouldn't ask for money. Your answer should be that the money is intended to support the child. The child's needs have not changed so why should the amount of support.

When applying for reimbursement of adoption expenses, start by getting the diagnosis to affirm special needs status. Then document everything. If the state or agency asks for an accounting, include every expense connected to the adoption that you can think of.

Hiring an Attorney

You need to be represented by your own expert. Because of many competing parties and positions, foster/adoptive parents should have their own attorney to help negotiate the above subsidies. Your interests differ from those of the state and any competing families in a contested adoption. Having your own attorney is especially critical where negotiations are involved.

When you are hiring your own attorney, ask what specific services he or she will provide and how much it will cost. Funds up to the NRAE amount allowed in your state are available to pay for your attorney. Get an attorney who is experienced and knowledgeable about foster care and adoption policies and subsidies. To find a good attorney, ask your fellow foster parents.

Appeal for a Fair Hearing

If the parents feel they have been treated unfairly by the

agency, or in an untimely manner, they can request an administrative hearing. The most common reasons include a reduction in the foster care or adoption subsidy rate without due notice or if the parents finalized an adoption of a special needs child without subsidy and believe the child is (and was) eligible. The right to pursue a fair hearing through appeals applies to other issues as well. If the parents are still not satisfied, they can appeal further to the court.

Summary

Foster-to-adopt parents are entitled to continuing support after the adoption. This may include a monthly per diem subsidy, medical insurance, reimbursement for expenses, a federal tax credit, and help later with college tuition. These entitlements should be established before the adoption is finalized. To assure maximum benefits for their child, adopting parents may profit from the services of a knowledgeable attorney in negotiating and in court.

9
TIPS ON DISCIPLINE
James A. Kenny, PhD

Parent: "Finish up your homework." The child responds by mumbling a vague assent but continues to watch TV. Parent responds with intermittent encouragement and reminding, pointing out how homework leads to good grades, and later, a good job. How important homework is. Child continues to procrastinate. The parent's voice gets louder.

The child may then make some smart-alecky comment, and the parent responds angrily: "That's it. To bed right now, and you're grounded from TV and the phone."

Too many parents use the L-Y-P method of discipline (Lecture-Yell-Punish). After some failure or misbehavior, the parent begins by explaining at length. The lecture deteriorates to nagging, and sometimes gives way to demanding and shouting by the parent. When that doesn't work, the parent may threaten and punish.

Here are twelve tips on getting children to mind. They are underscored by two important principles:

- ✧ **There is more to discipline than punishment.** Other better methods are available for obtaining compliance.
- ✧ **You will get more of whatever you pay attention to.** So don't waste your attention on misbehavior. Be brief, and when possible, ignore bad behavior. Behavior of any kind, including misbehavior, will not continue long without attention. Save most of your attention for good behavior.

1. Target good behavior. Identify the bad behavior and then focus on its opposite: the completion of chores and homework, going to bed on time, no bad language, the absence of disciplinary notes from the teacher.

2. Stay positive. Reward successes rather than punish failures or misbehavior. Research shows that punishing is a poor way to motivate. Why waste parental time and attention on behavior you want to stop? Instead, identify a bad behavior like fighting, foul language, or coming home late. Then reward its opposite: playing cooperatively, "happy mouth," or coming home on time.

3. Keep score on the calendar or with charts. Charting is a good way to get a new discipline plan started. Basketball coaches keep track of points scored, rebounds, and assists. Factory foremen keep statistics on each worker's production. Parents do well when they take "official notice" of each success and record it.

4. Be brief in responding to misbehavior. Lecturing and grounding are usually counter-productive for the simple reason that they take too long. The attention, even though negative, is perceived as a secondary gain and is often a reason why misbehavior goes on and on. Best to stop the misbehavior as abruptly as possible and find some way to respond to its opposite.

5. Be immediate. For rewards (or consequences) to be maximally effective, they need to happen at once. Parents could learn from big business which uses this concept effectively, with its immediate sales, premiums, and discounts.

6. Be physical. We do not mean spanking, but rather a whole range of effective non-verbal responses. Words take too long and provide secondary gain. It may help to imagine you have duct tape over your mouth. What can you do? Distract him. Have pre-planned games or activities. Go and get her. Separate combatants. Confiscate the cell phone or the car keys. Turn off the TV.

7. Be consistent. This does not mean parents cannot change their disciplinary goals. Consistency does mean that they should stick to their word, follow through, and agree with each other in implementing the consequences.

8. Focus on the outcome. Be concrete and specific and don't get lost in the processes of discipline. Select behaviors that can be observed and counted. Goals like "attitude" and "respect" are too vague and general. Instead, look to goals like coming home on time, the absence of certain unacceptable words, and teacher reports on completed assignments. Find quick and simple ways to achieve these goals.

9. Discipline can be fun. Wise parents can sometimes make discipline a game. If you want the room picked up, play "Beat the Clock" or "Beat the Song." If you want quiet, play "Shazaam!" Everyone who is quiet till you say "Pinocchio" gets one M&M. If kids are fighting, play "Magic Chair." Blow the whistle and everyone who goes to their previously agreed-upon chair until you blow the "all clear" whistle earns a tiny immediate surprise.

10. Set a good example. Be a model of the behavior you expect. Don't use words you don't want your kids to use. Don't shout at your spouse or kids. Don't smoke. Drive within the speed limit. Fasten your seatbelt.

11. Structure the environment. Post the house rules, including chore lists and curfew times for everyone. Have a written policy on phone use and abuse. If necessary, lock up money, valuables, and liquor. Do your own detective work and don't ask children to incriminate themselves. If you have reason to doubt where they say they will be, check for yourself.

12. Listen. Children will have important reasons for wanting what they want. Hear them out. When limits are set, children may well be angry. Listen, even if you think it's "backtalk." Stick to your ruling, but accept their resentment. Children, like all of us, need to learn how to express themselves civilly, and sometimes, how to lose their point.

Of course children fail to mind. Sometimes their behavior may be outrageous. That, however, is what parents are for, to teach and demonstrate the right way to do and behave, to get them ready them for a happy and productive adulthood. Good luck!

10
TREATING REACTIVE DETACHMENT DISORDER
James A. Kenny, PhD

All love ends in tragedy. People leave. People die. But not to love is the definition of hell. Some people are so devastated by loss that they "decide" that love is not worth the risk. One or two broken hearts are all they can handle. They "turn off" their yearning to give and receive affection. This is especially true of young people with minimal life experience. Even moreso, this is an occupational hazard of foster children.

Each one of us must deal with the dilemma of loving. To love and be loved is the paramount human experience. None of us are sufficient unto ourselves. We need one another. In fact, we were "made" by an act of love. In addition, the ability to feel love protects us from harming others. We have "com"passion, we feel "with." For these reasons, most of us decide that loving is worth the pain of loss.

This dilemma is endemic to foster care. Children are shifted around, drift back and forth to birth home and to other foster homes. No matter how cogent the reasons and how careful the explanations to the child that a move was unavoidable, the child's elemental feeling is one of rejection. "If you really loved me, you would keep me." The way a large number of foster children handle this is by not caring, by being unable or refusing to attach.

We foster parents also have a dilemma. Of course we get attached. I would not give a nickel for a foster parent who did not. Yet this poses two problems for foster parents. First, the child may be resistant to attachment no matter how hard we try to reach out to him. This is called "Reactive Attachment

Disorder" or RAD. And second, if we do become closely attached, are we setting the child up for another rejection when he or she is moved?

Reactive Attachment Disorder is a psychiatric diagnosis that identifies children suffering from severely disturbed and inappropriate patterns of relating. RAD may be expressed as a lack of concern for rights and needs of others or in a superficial and overly conforming attempt to please. RAD children typically fail to develop a conscience and do not learn to trust. Symptoms include stealing, lying about the obvious ('crazy' lying), cruelty to animals, a lack of impulse controls, and poor peer relationships.

A major cause of RAD appears to be a failure to form normal attachments to primary caregivers in early childhood. This might be the result of early experiences of neglect or abuse, abrupt separation from caregivers in the first three years, frequent change of caregivers, or a lack of caregiver responsiveness.

"Attachment" is a general term that indicates connectedness of one type or another. "Bonding" is a significant reciprocal attachment which both parties want and expect to continue, and which is interrupted at considerable peril to the persons involved.

How do we humans bond? All of us, children and adults, bond the same way, by sharing over time important events in daily life, such as eating, sleeping, and playing together. The research shows that bonding is likely after three months of daily contact, probable after six, and almost certain after twelve months. Unless you are a foster child with RAD. Then it may not happen at all. At this point, the reader might wish to review the earlier section on "Legal Definitions of Bonding."

What can be done for the unbonded child, the one suffering from RAD? Since bonding is a natural and normal human experience, the cure will take place in a home, not in a therapist's office. A wise therapist will work primarily with the parents, reviewing strategies for overcoming problems with attachment and encouraging the family to persevere.

The first task for the therapist is to do everything possible to help find a permanent home. Otherwise, the therapist and the family face an impossible dilemma. They want the child to attach and bond, but not have to face another damaging rejection if and when the child is moved again.

Once permanence has been achieved, here are five obvious and common sense strategies for the therapist to communicate to the beleaguered parents:

1. Be patient. Realize that bonding takes time. Rebonding takes more time. It will not happen overnight. It may take a year or more. It will not happen in a therapist's office. The unbonded child may show his lack of compassion in many ways, by not caring, by hurting other children, by being cruel to animals. Deal with these problems as best you can by preventing them. You will be tempted to judge him and even to give up. Stay the course.

2. Don't force him. He may resist a personal relationship for a long time. He may be quiet, appear bored, act as if he doesn't care. He may not respond to your love or show remorse for misbehavior. Continue to make overtures of caring and affection but do not overdo it. Let him attach at his own pace.

3. Pass the tests. He will put you to the test. He may misbehave or destroy things that you value to see if you really love him. Again, prevent this if you can. Tell him this has hurt you. But do not hurt him back. He needs your discipline but he also needs your unconditional love.

4. Be as good as your word. If you say you will do something, do it. If you tell him you will be home at a certain time, don't be late. If you get delayed, call him. Against the backdrop of regular letdowns, he needs to learn to begin trusting again. Consistency is key.

5. Be there. Don't worry too much if you lose your temper once in awhile or think you have made a mistake. We all do. Be present. Be available. In word and in touch. He needs to learn that you are his forever parent. No matter what he does, how much he strikes out, he needs to realize that you will always be there.

11

ALLEGATIONS HAPPEN:
HOW TO PREVENT AND SURVIVE THEM
from Spring 2002 Adoptalk by Diane Martin-Hushman

"It's the worst thing that's ever happened to me," said one parent about the time her foster daughter filed an abuse allegation against her. Most often false, allegations of abuse against parents who foster and adopt children with special needs are frighteningly common. When parenting these special children, it is in our best interest to prevent situations that could be construed as inappropriate, and seek out help when an allegation disrupts our lives.

Whether false or confirmed, allegations arise for different reasons. We hope that children who are abused by their caregivers will notify a teacher, social worker, or someone else in authority. But sometimes children whose backgrounds include abuse are highly sensitized to triggers that they associate with abuse. You may just be leading a child to a time out after he kicks his sister; but the instant you grab his arm, your foster son may flash back to times when he was dragged to a room and whipped with his birth father's belt. As children age through the foster care system, and grow in street wisdom and anger, many also learn that allegations are a ticket out of a placement, a means of getting attention, and a way to keep parents who are starting to get too close a safe distance away.

The general public is concerned about child abuse and neglect, but not very knowledgeable about how parents must try to deal with some very difficult behaviors presented by abused children. The media is quick to shine the spotlight on a few foster and adoptive parents who abuse children in their care, and say little about those who are diligently working to improve children's lives. Once they happen, allegations are hard to live down.

Consequences of Allegations

When I was a social worker, a 13-year-old girl in my caseload alleged that her 71-year-old foster grandfather had sexually abused her. The grandfather had a heart condition and I thought the reports would kill him! After looking into the charges, investigators discovered that the girl was distorting the situation and reenacting a previous abuse situation with her birth grandfather.

Though not substantiated, the charge became part of the family's case file, and the stress family members experienced lingered on. Many parents describe allegations and the subsequent investigation as a process of loss and grief. Parents may lose their sense of identity, their self-esteem, and their trust in the worker or agency. Children may be removed – another painful loss for both the children and parents. Even after child protection closes the case, a parent may feel that the family's good name is forever tarnished and the episode will never be resolved.

Allegations that uncover licensing violations or substantiated abuse claims can cause additional stress. Depending on the severity of the infraction, foster parents may be placed on probation, be issued a correction order, or have their license temporarily suspended or permanently revoked. Serious allegations may result in a criminal charge that could land a parent in jail, and forever ruin chances of fostering or adopting another child.

Allegation Prevention Strategies

Foster and adoptive families who have lots of children, including children of different races, and who have been fostering for a long time are at greater risk of being reported for alleged abuse. All families who care for children with special needs face some risk, and every parent can take steps to keep situations from turning into allegations. Below are some ideas for parents to consider.

⬦ **Know your limits.** If you are not comfortable handling children with certain challenging backgrounds and behaviors, don't set yourself up by bringing such children into your home.

⬦ **Learn all you can about each child before placement.** You have a right to know about previous abuse and allegations. Ask: "Has this child been abused? In what way? Who were the perpetrators? Have there been any abuse allegations?" Had the foster family whose 13-year-old girl charged the grandfather with abuse known about her abuse history, they would never have left the foster grandfather alone with her.

⬦ **Make sure that men and boys in your house are never alone with a girl who has been sexually abused.** Proactive precautions are very important in this situation, especially at the beginning of the placement. Talk with your partner and others in the household about this safety plan, and stay proactive.

⬦ **Give each sexually abused child his or her own bedroom.** I know this is difficult, but why put another child in your home at risk? If a child's boundaries have been invaded, he or she needs to re-learn proper boundaries.

⬦ **Be crystal clear about rules for dress, privacy, touching, etc.** Caregivers must agree on house rules, boundaries, and consequences. Each child comes from a different culture of parenting, sexuality, sleeping habits, dress, touch, and more, and needs to learn what is appropriate. As a foster mom, I talked about sexuality as one of the house rules. "In this house," I would say, "my husband gets his sexual needs met with me and only me." Sound crude? Yes, but I said it in a matter-of-fact way and set a very clear boundary that the teenage girls we worked with really needed.

✧ **Never use physical discipline.** Corporal punishment is not allowed in foster care, but I know some folks think that once the kids are adopted, physical discipline is okay. Don't do it. Children with a history of physical, sexual, or emotional abuse often misinterpret physical discipline and an allegation is likely. Physical discipline can also undermine attachment.

✧ **Avoid teasing, horseplay, wrestling, and suggestive language.** These are acts of intimacy, and intimacy is just what abused children often resist. In addition, the child may get a different message than you intend during the close physical contact involved.

✧ **Document sexual acting out in writing.** Send reports to the child's social worker and therapist. Then, if another incident comes to light, the worker and therapist can see that there might be a pattern to the child's acting out that perhaps relates to past experiences.

✧ **Document behavior patterns.** When a child enters your home, use a calendar to record changes in the child's behavior; inappropriate words or actions during birth parent visits; the child's behavior following visits; the cause of scratches, bruises, or other injuries; and any patterns of behavior that seem to follow specific events or times of the year (like anniversaries of certain past events).

✧ **Participate in a support group.** As foster and adoptive parents of children with special needs, we need to share the struggles and joys that are a part of our lives with those who can empathize and support us. We need folks who can laugh and cry with us and really understand foster and adoptive parents' journey.

✧ **Reserve personal time to reduce stress.** Know what really pushes your buttons, and establish a calming plan. Post twenty tips on calming on the refrigerator and model stress-reduction techniques for your children. Then, make plans for a weekly – yes, weekly – time away from the children. Take care of yourself; you are the child's greatest gift!

Allegation Survival Strategies

Sometimes, despite a family's efforts to prevent them, allegations will happen. Maybe things are going a little too well with Jimmy – a 12-year-old with a history of sexual abuse – and he starts to get scared. The week after a lively game of Twister with his foster dad, Jimmy tells his worker that the foster dad was touching and pressing his body against Jimmy's. Jimmy claims it was sexual abuse, and soon child protection opens a case file to investigate Jimmy's allegation.

The foster family is looking at weeks or months of investigation, and Jimmy moves to an emergency shelter. What can the parents do to take care of themselves?

- ✧ **Try to stay positive.** Assume that the charge will be proven false, and try not to presume guilt. Statistics I've seen say that about 65 to 70 percent of all allegations are false. Child protection has to investigate to make certain that the child is not being abused. The best thing you can do is cooperate.
- ✧ **Document everything.** Start a notebook to record details of every phone conversation, personal interview, and correspondence related to the allegation. Write in pen, and be prepared to use the notebook to back up your story in court if need be. Request copies of the written charge against your family, as well as the letter that formally states that the allegations were unfounded.
- ✧ **Educate yourself.** Insist on getting a copy of your state's foster care rules and laws pertaining to allegations and abuse, and learn about county or agency policies and procedures too. Find out what will happen during the investigation, what your rights are, and how you can appeal an investigator's determination.

✧ **Behave appropriately.** During interviews, make your point and then stop talking. Speak with confidence, and be factual, honest, respectful, and business like. Avoid emotional language when telling your side of the story. It may be extremely hard, but you must try to be objective.

✧ **Meet with people who are gathering information.** If an investigator asks to meet with you, don't keep her waiting. If you need to, bring along a friend or someone from your support group who can give you perspective on how the meeting went.

✧ **Communicate with your partner.** Allegations, especially those of sexual abuse, can really drive a wedge between partners. The husband thinks, "How could they think I would do something like that?!" The wife wonders, "Could it possibly be true?!" If not openly discussed, these questions can pull couples apart just when they need each other's support the most.

✧ **Know your rights.** Don't be afraid to appeal, request a waiver, and learn how the grievance procedure works. If need be, hire legal counsel. I would especially recommend hiring a good attorney for sexual abuse allegations.

What Support Groups Can Do to Help

In addition to counseling new foster and adoptive families about taking conscious steps to prevent allegations, support groups can be very helpful when a family is going through or has just concluded an allegation investigation. Sometimes, the best help is just being there. To support family members who are going through an investigation, a support group can:

✧ **Offer a sympathetic ear.** This is a time when families really need the support group! Make them feel welcome by respectfully listening.

✧ **Stay neutral.** It is not the group's job to fix the problem. There are many sides to the story, and the group should be objective. Agency bashing helps no one.

✧ **Share information.** Encourage members to talk about their experiences with allegations, and share local allegation policy and procedural information with the entire group.

✧ **Suggest resources.** Direct the family to legal services and suggest how they can obtain agency policies concerning allegations.

✧ **Assign a mentor.** Parents going through an allegation may have an easier time talking to one person who has experienced an allegation rather than the whole group. A call from someone who can say, "I've walked the walk," can mean so much during this time.

After the investigation is over, ask for help to regain your equilibrium, rebuild, and move on. Take really good care of yourself. Think hard and give yourself some time off before bringing a child back into your home, or accepting another placement. Take care of the children still in the home. Difficult times can be therapeutic and healing, showing children that we can have tough times, but as families we are strong and resilient. If you can't prevent an allegation, at least do what you can to survive, learn, and thrive.

12
FOSTER PARENT RESOURCES

Adoption in Child Time (ACT)
www.adoptioninchildtime.org
act4adoption@hotmail.com
815 Gardenbrook Circle, Unit D, Indianapolis, IN 46202

ACT is an advocacy group to promote early permanence for children in out-of-home care. Pursuing the timelines set by federal legislation, ACT provides information to agencies, attorneys, child welfare workers and foster parents about legislative and legal news. A year is a long time in the life of a child. ACT's motto recognizes the importance of avoiding unnecessary delays in achieving permanence.

AdoptUSKids - The Children's Bureau
www.adoptuskids.org

AdoptUSKids.org offers a national photo listing service for children awaiting adoption across the United States. You may "Meet the Children" by searching their photo listing.

Casey Family Programs
www.casey.org
(206) 282-7300
2001 Eighth Ave. Suite 2700, Seattle, WA 98121

Casey Family Programs' mission is to provide, improve, and ultimately to prevent the need for foster care. Established by United Parcel Service founder Jim Casey, they are a Seattle-based national foundation that has served children, youth, and families in the child welfare system since 1966. They operate in two ways. They provide direct services, and they promote advances in child-welfare practice and policy. They collaborate with foster, kinship, and adoptive parents to provide safe, loving homes for youth in our direct care. They also collaborate with counties, states, and American Indian and Alaska Native tribes to improve services and outcomes for the more than 500,000 young people in out-of-home care across the U.S.

Child Welfare League of America
www.cwla.org
cwla@cwla.org
(202) 688-4200
1726 M St. NW, Suite 500, Washington, DC, 20036

CWLA is a powerful coalition of hundreds of private and public agencies serving children and families that are vulnerable since 1920. Their expertise, leadership and innovation on policies, programs, and practices help improve the lives of millions of children across the country. CWLA leads and engages its network of public and private agencies and partners to advance policies, best practices and collaborative strategies that result in better outcomes for children, youth and families that are vulnerable.

Children's Bureau: U.S. Department of Health and Human Services
Administration on Children, Youth, and Families
www.acf.hhs.gov/programs/cb
1250 Maryland Ave., SW, Washington, D.C. 20024

The **Children's Bureau (CB)** is the oldest federal agency for children and is located within the United States Department of Health and Human Services' Administration for Children and Families. It is responsible for assisting states in the delivery of child welfare services - services designed to protect children and strengthen families. The agency provides grants to states, tribes and communities to operate a range of child welfare services including child protective services (child abuse and neglect), family preservation and support, foster care, adoption and independent living. In addition, the agency makes major investments in staff training, technology and innovative programs.

The **Child Welfare Information Gateway** connects child welfare and related professionals to comprehensive information and resources to help protect children and strengthen families. They feature the latest on topics from prevention to permanency, including child abuse and neglect, foster care, and adoption.

The **Adoption and Foster Care Analysis and Reporting System (AFCARS)** collects case-level information from state and tribal title IV-E agencies on all children in foster care and those who have been adopted with title IV-E agency involvement. Title IV-E agencies are required to submit AFCARS data semi-annually to the Children's Bureau.

Dave Thomas Foundation for Adoption
www.davethomasfoundationforadoption.org
info@davethomasfoundation.org
(800) 275-3832
716 Mt. Airyshire Blvd., Suite 100, Columbus, OH 43235

At the Dave Thomas Foundation for Adoption, they believe they have a responsibility to be the voice of foster care adoption, so that every child finds a family. They attempt to find homes for children who are waiting to be adopted from foster care in North America. In the process, they work to inform adults who may have misperceptions about foster care adoption that keep them from getting involved. Through the money they raise, they are able to provide free educational resources, promote awareness, assist policymakers and employers, and support adoption professionals and agencies throughout the United States and Canada to ensure that every child finds a forever home.

Foster Family Treatment Association
www.ffta.org
(800) 414-3382
294 Union Street, Hackensack, NJ 07601

FFTA members are well represented nationally through long-standing relationships and on-going collaborations with the White House, Center for Medicare and Medicaid Policy, SAMHSA, HHS, congressional offices and committees of both the House and the Senate, and a broad coalition of national and state child welfare and child advocacy organizations. Policy endeavors in which they are involved include: legislation for a national definition of treatment foster care, child welfare reform, domestic minor sex trafficking, mental health and psychotropic medications for foster youth, relative and kinship care, and community systems-of-care. FFTA is committed to enhancing the lives of children within families through strengthening family-based organizations.

Fostering Families Today Magazine
Adoption Today & Fostering Families Today Magazines
www.fosteringfamiliestoday.com
(888-924-6736)
541 E Garden Dr Unit N, Windsor, CO 80550

National bimonthly magazines by and about foster and adoptive parents.

National Foster Parent Association (NFPA)
www.nfpaonline.org
info@nfpaonline.org
(800) 557-5238

The National Foster Parent Association (NFPA) is a nonprofit, volunteer organization established in 1972. The purpose of NFPA is to bring together foster parents, agency representatives and community people who wish to work together to improve the foster care system and enhance the lives of all children and families; to promote mutual coordination, cooperation and communication among foster parents, foster parent associations, child care agencies and other child advocates; and to encourage the recruitment and retention of foster parents.

North American Council on Adoptable Children (NACAC)

www.nacac.org
info@nacac.org
(651) 644-3036
970 Raymond Avenue, Suite 106, St. Paul, MN 55114

Founded in 1974 by adoptive parents, the North American Council on Adoptable Children is committed to meeting the needs of waiting children and the families who adopt them. Since its inception, NACAC's mission has remained essentially unchanged. The Council advocates the right of every child to a permanent, continuous, nurturing and culturally sensitive family.

NACAC is the premier source for information on adoption subsidies and the tax credit nationally and state by state. They will answer individual questions from foster and adoptive parents.

Voice for Adoption (VFA)

www.voice-for-adoption.org
(202) 210-8118
1220 L Street NW
Suite 100-344
Washington, DC 20005

VFA develops and advocates for improved adoption policies. VFA works closely with federal and state legislators, as well as other child welfare organizations, to make a difference in the lives of the 107,000 children in foster care who are waiting to be adopted and the families who adopt children from foster care.

You Gotta Believe
www.yougottabelieve.org
info@yougottabelieve.org
(718) 372-3003
3114 Mermaid Ave, Brooklyn, NY, 11224

You Gotta Believe! (The Older Child Adoption and Permanency Movement, Inc.) is an IRS determined 501(c)(3) not-for-profit corporation and was approved by the State of New York to have the authority to both place out and board out children since 1995. They seek to prevent homelessness by finding permanent moral and legal adoptive homes for teens and preteen children in foster care.

ABOUT ADOPTION IN CHILD TIME

WHO WE ARE AND WHAT WE DO

ACT is an Indiana-based advocacy group which:
✧ Promotes early permanence for children in out-of-home care.
✧ Pursues the objectives set out by the Adoption and Safe Families Act
✧ Informs agencies, attorneys, child welfare workers and foster parents about legislative and legal news.
✧ Advocates for legislation which advances the goal of early permanence.
✧ Presents objective information on child placement issues for use by agencies and courts.

WHAT YOU'LL FIND ON ACT'S WEB SITE,

www.adoptioninchildtime.org

✧ Pamphlets and articles available for downloading such as the following:
✧ Treating reactive attachment disorder
✧ When siblings should and should not be separated
✧ How foster parents can and should advocate for their foster children
✧ The importance of bonding
✧ When foster parents need an attorney
✧ Subsidy and tax issues
✧ How to present bonding and attachment issues in court
✧ And much more!

ACT BOOKS ARE AVAILABLE ON AMAZON.COM

Attachment and Bonding in the Foster and Adopted Child (2014)

James Kenny, PhD and Peter Kenny, JD

- ✧ Foster parents will learn how to make their voice heard in case conferences and in court.

- ✧ Birth parents will learn effective strategies for reunification.

- ✧ Adoptive parents will learn how to weave a path through the many laws and polices involved, and how to obtain the subsidies available.

- ✧ Mental health professionals will learn how to evaluate bonding in four objective and verifiable definitions that can be presented in court.

- ✧ Case managers will learn how and why the child's needs are paramount, and how to engage the older child in planning for his or her future.

- ✧ Child welfare administrators will learn innovative recommendations about ways to improve the system and reduce time in foster care.

- ✧ Attorneys will learn how to help foster parents advocate for their wards, defend them against allegations, and argue their case in a contested adoption.

- ✧ All readers will learn why bonded relationships are so important and how their disruption leads to significant increases in mental illness, crime, and homelessness.

What Foster Parents Need to Know: Keeping a Journal, Handling Allegations, Adoption Subsidies, and More (2015)

The content in the book you are reading was compiled and written by the following:

Peter Kenny, after graduating from Indiana University Law School in 1997, has devoted his legal practice to representing foster parents on a variety of issues, especially for those who wish to provide permanent homes to children through adoption. He is the co-founder in 1998 and Executive Director of ACT and has successfully lobbied for significant changes in Indiana laws which have strengthened foster parents' rights. He has offered dozens of workshops and seminars to attorneys, caseworkers, health care professionals, and foster parents. Kenny is the author of three books: *Attachment and Bonding in the Foster and Adopted Child, Adopting a Foster Child,* and *The Right to a Permanent Home.*

Mark Bontrager is the Executive Director of Aldea, a large child care agency in Napa, California. He is also an ACSW social worker and licensed attorney and has co-authored ACT's A Daily Journal for Foster Parents.

James Kenny has doctorates in Clinical Psychology and in Anthropology plus an MSW. He has published articles in numerous professional journals and popular magazines and authored books on family and child care, including *Whole Life Parenting,* and *Parenting Tomorrow's Child.*

He and his wife have raised 12 children, four of whom are adopted. In addition, they were licensed foster parents, primarily caring for teenage boys.

Tom and Jean Gaunt. Tom is an engineer in Indianapolis, managing director of Geometric Solutions. Jean is a special education teacher. More importantly, they are longtime foster parents and adoptive parents of eleven, including a family of nine. The latter story was featured in the award-winning documentary A Place Called Home. They also authored *Why and How to Prepare a Life Book.*

Diane Martin-Hushman, MSW, is the Parent Group Coordinator for the North American Council on Adoptable Children. Her experiences as a foster and adoptive parent have made her passionately committed to adoptive parent support groups.

How to Contact Us

Website: www.adoptioninchildtime.org
E-mail: act4adoption@hotmail.com
Jim Kenny, Board President
Post: 815-D Gardenbrook Circle, Indianapolis, IN 46202